Flavors of the Grill

A Crispy BBQ Chicken Wings Adventure

While every precaution has been taken in the preparation of this book, the publisher assumes no responsibility for errors or omissions, or for damages resulting from the use of the information contained herein.

FLAVORS OF THE GRILL

First edition. January 5, 2024.

ISBN: 979-8224346837

Written by Jose Maria.

Table of Contents

Jose Maria

❖ Introduction

A. Welcome and Brief Overview

Welcome to the sizzling world of "Flavors of the Grill: A Crispy BBQ Chicken Wings Adventure"! Today, we're delving into the art of creating mouthwatering BBQ chicken wings that are crispy, flavorful, and downright irresistible.

B. Why BBQ Chicken Wings?

Why do we find ourselves drawn to the allure of BBQ chicken wings? It's more than just a dish; it's an experience. The combination of smoky flavors, tender meat, and the satisfying crunch of perfectly crispy skin makes BBQ chicken wings a culinary masterpiece. Join us on this journey as we unlock the secrets to mastering this beloved classic.

C. Tips for Perfectly Crispy Wings

Crispiness is the holy grail of BBQ chicken wings, and we've got the insider tips to make sure your wings achieve the perfect crunch. From selecting the finest ingredients to mastering cooking techniques, we'll guide you through every step. Get ready to elevate your wing game and leave everyone craving for more. Let's dive in!

Chapter (1) Getting Started

A. Ingredients
Chicken Wings

- 2-3 pounds of fresh, high-quality chicken wings for optimal flavor and succulence.

BBQ Sauce

- 1 cup of your favorite BBQ sauce. Choose a brand you love or experiment with homemade variations for a personalized touch.

Marinade and Rub
Marinade:

- 1/4 cup soy sauce
- 2 cloves garlic, minced
- 1 tablespoon olive oil
- 1 teaspoon Worcestershire sauce

Dry Rub:

- 2 tablespoons paprika
- 1 teaspoon cayenne pepper (adjust for spice preference)
- 2 tablespoons brown sugar
- 1 teaspoon salt
- Optional Dipping Sauces

Choose from:

- Classic Ranch
- Creamy Blue Cheese
- Zesty Aioli

B. Equipment
Grill

- Whether gas or charcoal, ensure it's in good working condition for optimal grilling.

Oven

- Preheat to 400°F (200°C) for baking, or use the broil setting for a finishing touch.

Basting Brush

- A silicone brush for applying marinade and glaze evenly on the wings.

Baking Sheet

- A large baking sheet to accommodate the wings for oven baking.

Tongs

- Sturdy tongs for flipping and handling the wings on the grill or in the oven.

Gathering these key ingredients and equipment is the first step to a successful BBQ chicken wing adventure. Now, let's move on to preparing the wings for a flavor-packed experience!

Chapter (2) Preparing the Wings

A. Cleaning and Trimming

- Start with fresh chicken wings, ensuring they are clean and free from any feathers or unwanted particles.
- Trim excess fat and loose skin from the wings using kitchen shears. This not only enhances the aesthetic appeal but also helps the wings cook more evenly.

B. Marinating

In a bowl, combine the marinade ingredients:

- **1/4 cup soy sauce**
- **2 cloves garlic, minced**
- **1 tablespoon olive oil**
- **1 teaspoon Worcestershire sauce**

- Place the cleaned and trimmed chicken wings in a large resealable plastic bag or a shallow dish.
- Pour the marinade over the wings, ensuring each piece is well-coated. Seal the bag or cover the dish with plastic wrap.
- Allow the wings to marinate in the refrigerator for at least 2 hours, or ideally, overnight. This time allows the flavors to penetrate the meat, resulting in a more flavorful outcome.

C. Applying the Rub

In a separate bowl, mix the dry rub ingredients:

- **2 tablespoons paprika**
- **1 teaspoon cayenne pepper (adjust to taste)**
- **2 tablespoons brown sugar**
- **1 teaspoon salt**

- After marinating, remove the wings from the refrigerator and let them come to room temperature for about 30 minutes.
- Preheat your grill or oven according to the chosen cooking method.
- Pat the wings dry with paper towels to ensure a crispy skin. Sprinkle the dry rub over the wings, coating them evenly. Massage the rub into the wings to ensure it adheres well.

Your wings are now prepped and infused with flavor. Whether you choose to grill or bake, the next steps will guide you towards achieving that perfect crispiness we're aiming for in this BBQ chicken wings adventure!

Chapter (3) Cooking Methods

A. Grilling
Direct vs. Indirect Heat

- Direct Heat: Place the marinated and rubbed wings directly over the hot coals or flames. Sear them for 2-3 minutes per side to lock in juices and create a flavorful outer layer.
- Indirect Heat: Move the wings to the cooler side of the grill or turn off burners beneath them. Continue cooking with the grill lid closed, allowing the wings to cook through without direct heat. This step prevents flare-ups and ensures a thorough cook.

Timing and Temperature

- Grill Temperature: Maintain a consistent grill temperature of around 375°F (190°C).
- Timing: Grill the wings for a total of 20-25 minutes, turning them every 5 minutes with tongs for even cooking. Check for doneness by using a meat thermometer – the internal temperature should reach 165°F (74°C).

B. Oven-Baking
Baking vs. Broiling

- Baking: Preheat your oven to 400°F (200°C). Place a wire rack on a baking sheet to elevate the wings and allow excess fat to drip away, promoting crispiness. Bake for 45-50 minutes, turning the wings halfway through for an even golden brown finish.
- Broiling: For the last 5 minutes, switch your oven to the broil setting. Keep a close eye on the wings to prevent burning. This intense heat at the end enhances the crispiness of the skin.

Achieving Crispy Skin

- Elevating on a Wire Rack: Placing the wings on a wire rack ensures air circulation around each piece, preventing the underside from becoming soggy.
- Temperature Adjustment: If you choose not to broil, consider increasing the oven temperature slightly in the last 5-10 minutes to achieve that perfect crispy skin without compromising the juiciness of the meat.

With your wings expertly cooked, it's time to move on to the next phase – basting and glazing – to infuse them with layers of mouthwatering flavor!

Chapter (4) Basting and Glazing

A. Importance of Basting

Basting is a crucial step in the BBQ chicken wing journey, enhancing flavor, moisture, and that delectable glossy finish. Regularly applying a flavorful liquid during the cooking process not only prevents the wings from drying out but also builds layers of taste. Get ready to elevate your wings to new heights!

B. DIY BBQ Sauce Recipes

Classic Tangy BBQ

Ingredients:

- 1 cup ketchup
- 1/2 cup apple cider vinegar
- 1/4 cup molasses
- 1/4 cup brown sugar
- 1 tablespoon Dijon mustard
- 1 teaspoon smoked paprika
- 1/2 teaspoon garlic powder
- Salt and pepper to taste

Instructions:

- In a saucepan, combine all ingredients over medium heat.
- Bring to a simmer, stirring frequently.
- Reduce heat and let it simmer for 15-20 minutes until the sauce thickens.
- Adjust seasoning to taste.

Sweet and Spicy

Ingredients:

- 1 cup ketchup

- **1/3 cup honey**
- **1/4 cup soy sauce**
- **2 tablespoons Sriracha sauce (adjust for spice preference)**
- **1 tablespoon brown sugar**
- **1 teaspoon garlic powder**
- **1/2 teaspoon ginger, grated**

Instructions:

- In a bowl, whisk together all ingredients until well combined.
- Taste and adjust the sweetness or spiciness according to your preference.
- Honey Mustard Glaze

Ingredients:

- **1/2 cup Dijon mustard**
- **1/4 cup honey**
- **2 tablespoons mayonnaise**
- **1 tablespoon lemon juice**
- **Salt and pepper to taste**

Instructions:

- In a bowl, whisk together Dijon mustard, honey, mayonnaise, and lemon juice until smooth.
- Season with salt and pepper to taste.

Choose one or mix and match these sauces to baste your wings during the last 10 minutes of cooking. The result? Wings that are not only crispy on the outside but bursting with rich, flavorful goodness on the inside. Let's continue this culinary adventure with serving suggestions and side dishes!

Chapter (5) Serving Suggestions

A. Presentation Tips

Platter Arrangement:

Arrange the crispy BBQ chicken wings on a large platter, creating an inviting display that showcases their golden-brown perfection.

Garnish with Fresh Herbs:

Sprinkle chopped fresh parsley or cilantro over the wings for a burst of color and a touch of herbal freshness.

Serve with Lemon Wedges:

Place lemon wedges on the platter for a zesty, citrusy element that complements the richness of the wings.

Dipping Sauce Bowls:

Arrange small bowls with your chosen dipping sauces (Ranch, Blue Cheese, or Zesty Aioli) strategically around the platter for easy access.

B. Side Dishes
Coleslaw
Ingredients:

- **4 cups shredded cabbage and carrots (pre-packaged coleslaw mix works well)**
- **1/2 cup mayonnaise**
- **2 tablespoons apple cider vinegar**
- **1 tablespoon sugar**
- **Salt and pepper to taste**

Instructions:

- In a large bowl, whisk together mayonnaise, apple cider vinegar, sugar, salt, and pepper.
- Add shredded cabbage and carrots to the bowl, tossing until well-coated.
- Refrigerate for at least 30 minutes before serving.
- Corn on the Cob

Ingredients:

- **Fresh corn on the cob**
- **Butter**
- **Salt and pepper**

Instructions:

- Boil or grill the corn until tender.
- Brush with melted butter and sprinkle with salt and pepper before serving.
- Garlic Parmesan Fries

Ingredients:

- **Frozen or fresh-cut fries**
- **2 tablespoons olive oil**
- **2 cloves garlic, minced**
- **1/4 cup grated Parmesan cheese**
- **Salt and parsley for garnish**

Instructions:

- Bake or fry the fries according to package instructions.
- In a pan, sauté minced garlic in olive oil until fragrant.
- Toss the cooked fries in the garlic-infused oil.
- Sprinkle with grated Parmesan, salt, and chopped parsley.

Pair these delectable side dishes with your crispy BBQ chicken wings, creating a feast that tantalizes the taste buds. Let's move on to troubleshooting tips to ensure your wings turn out perfect every time!

Chapter (6) Troubleshooting

A. Overcooking/Undercooking

Overcooking:

If your wings are turning dry or too crispy, reduce the cooking time and monitor them closely, especially during the final stages.

Use a meat thermometer to ensure the internal temperature reaches 165°F (74°C) without surpassing it.

Undercooking:

If the wings are undercooked, extend the cooking time gradually, ensuring the internal temperature reaches the recommended 165°F (74°C).

For a crispier finish, you can always adjust by giving them a bit more time under direct heat or broiling.

B. Tips for Avoiding Soggy Skin

Elevate on a Wire Rack:

Placing the wings on a wire rack while baking or grilling allows air circulation, preventing the skin from becoming soggy.

Pat Dry Before Cooking:

Before applying the rub or placing them on the grill, pat the marinated wings dry with paper towels. Excess moisture can lead to soggy skin.

Adjust Oven Temperature:

If baking, ensure your oven is preheated properly. You can also increase the temperature slightly during the last few minutes for an extra crisp finish.

Avoid Crowding:

Whether on the grill or in the oven, avoid overcrowding the cooking space. This allows heat to circulate more efficiently around each wing.

C. Adjusting Flavors

Too Salty:

If the wings turn out too salty, counterbalance by serving them with a cooling dip like tzatziki or yogurt-based sauce.

Not Flavorful Enough:

Increase the quantity of your dry rub or marinade ingredients during preparation for a more robust flavor.

Balancing Spices:

If your wings are too spicy, add a touch of sweetness with a honey glaze during the final minutes of cooking. Conversely, if they lack heat, sprinkle a bit of cayenne pepper or hot sauce.

Sauce Adjustment:

If your BBQ sauce is too intense, dilute it with a bit of water or add a touch of honey for sweetness. For a bolder flavor, simmer the sauce to concentrate its taste.

With these troubleshooting tips, you'll be able to navigate any challenges and ensure your crispy BBQ chicken wings are a triumph of flavor and texture. Let's explore some exciting variations to keep the adventure going!

Chapter (7) Variations

A. Smoked BBQ Wings

Brining Process:

Before smoking, consider brining the wings for added moisture. Create a simple brine with water, salt, sugar, and aromatics like garlic and bay leaves. Let the wings soak in the brine for at least 4 hours.

Wood Chip Selection:

Choose wood chips that complement the smoky flavor, such as hickory or applewood. Soak them in water for at least 30 minutes before adding them to the smoker.

Low and Slow:

Smoke the wings at a lower temperature (around 225°F or 107°C) for a more extended period, allowing the smoky flavor to penetrate the meat. Aim for 2-3 hours of smoking time.

Basting with Mop Sauce:

Prepare a mop sauce with apple cider vinegar, olive oil, and your favorite BBQ rub. Baste the wings every hour during the smoking process to keep them moist and flavorful.

B. Asian-inspired Glazes

Teriyaki Glaze:

Mix soy sauce, honey, garlic, ginger, and a splash of rice vinegar for a classic teriyaki glaze. Brush this sweet and savory concoction on the wings during the last 10 minutes of grilling or baking.

Sesame Ginger Glaze:

Create a glaze using soy sauce, sesame oil, honey, minced ginger, and a sprinkle of sesame seeds. Brush the wings with this glaze while they cook, adding layers of Asian-inspired goodness.

Spicy Sriracha Glaze:

Combine Sriracha, soy sauce, honey, and lime juice for a zesty glaze. Adjust the spice level to your liking and brush it onto the wings for a bold and flavorful kick.

C. Dry Rub Variations

Cajun Spice Rub:

Mix paprika, onion powder, garlic powder, thyme, oregano, cayenne pepper, and a touch of brown sugar for a Cajun-inspired dry rub. Massage this blend onto the wings before grilling or baking.

Lemon Pepper Rub:

Combine lemon zest, black pepper, garlic powder, onion powder, and a pinch of salt. Sprinkle this refreshing rub on the wings for a bright and citrusy flavor.

Maple Bourbon Rub:

Create a rub with brown sugar, smoked paprika, salt, black pepper, and a hint of ground cinnamon. Add a tablespoon of bourbon and a drizzle of maple syrup to enhance the sweetness and depth of flavor.

Feel free to mix and match these variations or use them as inspiration to create your own signature twist on crispy BBQ chicken wings. The possibilities are endless! As we conclude, let's recap the key points and encourage you to embrace the joy of experimentation in your culinary endeavors.

Chapter (8) Appetizer Inspiration

A. Buffalo Chicken Dip

Ingredients:

- 2 cups cooked and shredded BBQ chicken
- 8 oz cream cheese, softened
- 1/2 cup ranch dressing
- 1/2 cup buffalo sauce
- 1 cup shredded cheddar cheese
- Green onions, chopped (for garnish)
- Tortilla chips or celery sticks (for dipping)

Instructions:

- Preheat the oven to 350°F (175°C).
- In a mixing bowl, combine shredded chicken, cream cheese, ranch dressing, buffalo sauce, and half of the shredded cheddar cheese.
- Transfer the mixture to a baking dish and top with the remaining cheddar cheese.
- Bake for 25-30 minutes or until the dip is hot and bubbly.
- Garnish with chopped green onions and serve with tortilla chips or celery sticks.

B. Stuffed Jalapeños with BBQ Chicken
Ingredients:

- 12 large jalapeños, halved and seeds removed
- 2 cups cooked and shredded BBQ chicken
- 8 oz cream cheese, softened
- 1 cup shredded cheddar cheese
- 1 teaspoon garlic powder
- 1 teaspoon onion powder
- Bacon slices (optional for wrapping)

Instructions:

- Preheat the oven to 375°F (190°C).
- In a bowl, combine shredded chicken, cream cheese, cheddar cheese, garlic powder, and onion powder.
- Stuff each jalapeño half with the chicken and cheese mixture.
- If desired, wrap each stuffed jalapeño with a slice of bacon and secure with toothpicks.
- Arrange on a baking sheet and bake for 20-25 minutes or until the jalapeños are tender and the filling is bubbly.

C. Chicken Wing Sliders
Ingredients:

- BBQ chicken wings (previously prepared)
- Slider buns
- Coleslaw (previously prepared)
- Pickles, for topping

Instructions:

- Take your pre-cooked and sauced BBQ chicken wings.

- Place a few wings on each slider bun.
- Top with a generous spoonful of coleslaw for a refreshing crunch.
- Add a pickle slice on top for an extra layer of flavor.
- Secure with toothpicks and serve as a delightful finger-food appetizer.

These appetizers are perfect for sharing and will complement your crispy BBQ chicken wings in creating a diverse and flavorful spread for your gathering. Enjoy the culinary journey!

Chapter (9) Marinade Madness

A. Citrus-infused Marinade
Ingredients:

- 1/2 cup orange juice
- Zest of 1 lemon
- Zest of 1 lime
- 2 tablespoons soy sauce
- 2 tablespoons olive oil
- 2 cloves garlic, minced
- 1 teaspoon cumin
- Salt and pepper to taste

Instructions:

- In a bowl, whisk together orange juice, lemon zest, lime zest, soy sauce, olive oil, minced garlic, cumin, salt, and pepper.
- Place the chicken wings in a resealable bag and pour the citrus-infused marinade over them.
- Seal the bag, ensuring the wings are well-coated, and refrigerate for at least 2 hours or overnight.

B. Beer and Honey Soak
Ingredients:

- 1 cup beer (choose a light lager or ale)
- 1/4 cup honey
- 2 tablespoons Dijon mustard
- 1 tablespoon apple cider vinegar
- 1 teaspoon smoked paprika
- Salt and pepper to taste

Instructions:

- In a bowl, combine beer, honey, Dijon mustard, apple cider vinegar, smoked paprika, salt, and pepper.
- Whisk until well blended.
- Submerge the chicken wings in the beer and honey marinade, ensuring they are well-covered.
- Allow the wings to marinate in the refrigerator for at least 2 hours, or overnight for a more intense flavor.

C. Teriyaki Twist
Ingredients:

- **1/2 cup soy sauce**
- **1/4 cup mirin (Japanese sweet rice wine)**
- **2 tablespoons honey**
- **1 tablespoon sesame oil**
- **2 cloves garlic, minced**
- **1 teaspoon grated ginger**
- **1 green onion, finely chopped**
- **Sesame seeds for garnish**

Instructions:

- In a bowl, whisk together soy sauce, mirin, honey, sesame oil, minced garlic, grated ginger, and chopped green onion.
- Pour the teriyaki marinade over the chicken wings in a resealable bag.
- Seal the bag and marinate in the refrigerator for at least 2 hours or overnight.
- Garnish with sesame seeds before serving.

Get ready for a burst of flavor with these diverse marinades. Whichever you choose, your wings are sure to be a hit at any gathering!

Chapter (10) Wing Hacks and Pro Tips

A. Using Baking Powder for Extra CrispinessIngredients:

- **Chicken wings**
- **Baking powder**
- **Salt and pepper (to taste)**

Instructions:

- After applying the rub, dust the wings with a light coating of baking powder. This helps draw moisture to the surface, creating a drier skin for enhanced crispiness.
- Ensure the wings are patted dry before applying the baking powder.
- Bake or grill the wings as usual, and enjoy the extra crispy texture.

B. The Perfect Beer Pairing

Light and Crisp Beers:

Pair your BBQ chicken wings with light and crisp beers like lagers or pilsners. Their refreshing qualities complement the smoky and savory flavors of the wings without overpowering them.

Hoppy IPAs:

For those who enjoy hoppy brews, an IPA can stand up well to the bold flavors of BBQ wings. The hop bitterness can cut through the richness of the wings, creating a delightful balance.

Dark and Malty Beers:

Opt for dark and malty beers like stouts or porters if you prefer a richer beer experience. These beers can provide a complementary depth to the BBQ flavors.

C. Grilling Secrets from Pitmasters

Preheat the Grill:

Allow your grill to preheat adequately before placing the wings. A hot grill ensures a good initial sear, locking in juices and flavor.

Clean and Oil the Grates:

Clean grates prevent sticking and ensure even cooking. Before grilling, brush the grates with oil to create a non-stick surface.

Two-Zone Grilling:

Create two zones on your grill – one for direct heat and one for indirect heat. Start with direct heat to sear the wings, then move them to the indirect zone to finish cooking without burning.

Wood Chips for Flavor:

Add soaked wood chips to your charcoal or gas grill for an extra layer of smoky flavor. Experiment with different wood varieties to customize the taste.

Use a Thermometer:

Invest in a meat thermometer to ensure precise cooking. The wings are ready when they reach an internal temperature of 165°F (74°C).

Rest Before Serving:

Allow the wings to rest for a few minutes after cooking. This helps redistribute juices, ensuring each bite is moist and flavorful.

Incorporate these wing hacks and pro tips into your BBQ chicken wing preparation to take your culinary skills to the next level. Now, it's time to enjoy the delicious fruits of your labor!

Chapter (11) Healthier Alternatives

A. Baked vs. Fried Options

Baked Wings:

Choose the baking method to reduce the amount of added fats and calories. Baking allows the wings to become crispy without the need for deep frying.

Elevate the wings on a wire rack while baking to allow excess fat to drip away, promoting a healthier outcome.

Air Fryer:

Utilize an air fryer for a healthier alternative to deep frying. The air fryer uses hot air circulation to create a crispy exterior with minimal oil.

Healthier Coating Options:

Instead of a traditional flour-based coating, consider using almond flour or a mixture of herbs and spices to add flavor and texture without excess calories.

B. Low-Sugar BBQ Sauces
Homemade BBQ Sauce:

Create your own BBQ sauce using natural sweeteners like honey, maple syrup, or agave nectar. This allows you to control the sugar content while still achieving a delightful sweetness.

Reduced-Sugar Store-Bought Options:

Choose store-bought BBQ sauces labeled as "low-sugar" or "sugar-free." These alternatives often use sugar substitutes or reduced amounts of sugar for a healthier option.

Fruit-Based Sauces:

Experiment with fruit-based sauces using ingredients like pureed berries or apples. These add natural sweetness without relying heavily on refined sugars.

C. Gluten-Free and Keto-Friendly Adjustments

Gluten-Free Coating:

Opt for gluten-free alternatives such as almond flour, coconut flour, or a mixture of gluten-free breadcrumbs and herbs for coating the wings.

Keto-Friendly BBQ Sauces:

Make or choose BBQ sauces with low-carb sweeteners like stevia or erythritol. This ensures your wings remain keto-friendly without compromising flavor.

Cauliflower Wings:

Experiment with cauliflower wings as a low-carb and gluten-free alternative. Coat cauliflower florets in a keto-friendly batter, bake or air fry until crispy, and toss in your preferred sauce.

Dipping Sauces:

Create keto-friendly dipping sauces using mayonnaise, sour cream, or Greek yogurt as a base. Add herbs, spices, and vinegar for extra flavor without the carbs.

By incorporating these healthier alternatives, you can still enjoy the deliciousness of BBQ chicken wings while aligning with specific dietary preferences or health-conscious choices. Feel free to get creative and adapt these suggestions to suit your individual needs!

Chapter (12) Global Wing Flavors

A. Caribbean Jerk Wings
  Jerk Marinade:

- 1/4 cup soy sauce
- 2 tablespoons olive oil
- 2 tablespoons brown sugar
- 2 tablespoons fresh thyme, chopped
- 2 green onions, chopped
- 2 cloves garlic, minced
- 1 tablespoon ginger, grated
- 1 tablespoon allspice
- 1 teaspoon cinnamon
- 1 teaspoon nutmeg
- 1 teaspoon cayenne pepper (adjust to taste)
- Salt and pepper to taste

Instructions:

- In a blender or food processor, combine all marinade ingredients and blend until smooth.
- Marinate the chicken wings for at least 2 hours, or preferably overnight.
- Grill or bake the wings until fully cooked, and enjoy the bold and spicy flavors of the Caribbean.

B. Tandoori Spiced Wings
  Tandoori Marinade:

- 1 cup plain yogurt

- 2 tablespoons tandoori spice blend
- 1 tablespoon ginger, minced
- 1 tablespoon garlic, minced
- 1 tablespoon lemon juice
- 1 teaspoon ground cumin
- 1 teaspoon ground coriander
- 1/2 teaspoon cayenne pepper (adjust to taste)
- Salt to taste

Instructions:

- In a bowl, mix all the tandoori marinade ingredients until well combined.
- Coat the chicken wings in the marinade, ensuring they are well-covered, and refrigerate for at least 4 hours or overnight.
- Grill or bake the wings until the internal temperature reaches 165°F (74°C), delivering a taste of India with every bite.

C. Mexican Mole Wings
Mole Sauce:

- 2 dried ancho chilies, seeded and stemmed
- 2 dried guajillo chilies, seeded and stemmed
- 3 tomatoes, roasted
- 1/2 cup almonds, toasted
- 1/4 cup raisins
- 3 cloves garlic
- 1 small onion, chopped and sautéed
- 1/4 cup sesame seeds, toasted
- 1/4 teaspoon cinnamon
- 1/4 teaspoon ground cloves
- 1/4 teaspoon ground coriander
- 1/4 teaspoon ground cumin

- **Salt and pepper to taste**

Instructions:

- In a blender, combine all mole sauce ingredients and blend until smooth.
- Simmer the mole sauce in a pan until it thickens, about 15-20 minutes.
- Toss the cooked chicken wings in the mole sauce until well-coated, and serve with a sprinkle of sesame seeds.

These globally inspired wing flavors bring a taste of the Caribbean, India, and Mexico to your table. Enjoy the journey around the world with these deliciously diverse chicken wing recipes!

Chapter (13) Leftover Remix

A. BBQ Chicken Wing Tacos
Ingredients:

- **Leftover BBQ chicken wings**
- **Small taco-sized tortillas**
- **Shredded lettuce**
- **Diced tomatoes**
- **Sliced red onions**
- **Chopped cilantro**
- **Lime wedges**
- **Sour cream or Greek yogurt (optional)**

Instructions:

- Remove the meat from the leftover wings, discarding the bones.
- Warm the tortillas and fill them with the shredded chicken.
- Top with shredded lettuce, diced tomatoes, sliced red onions, and chopped cilantro.
- Squeeze lime juice over the top and add a dollop of sour cream or Greek yogurt if desired.

Enjoy your flavorful BBQ chicken wing tacos!

B. Wing-Stuffed Baked Potatoes

Ingredients:

- **Leftover BBQ chicken wings**
- **Baked potatoes**
- **Butter**
- **Sour cream**
- **Shredded cheddar cheese**
- **Chopped green onions**
- **Salt and pepper to taste**

Instructions:

- Cut open the baked potatoes and fluff the insides with a fork.
- Remove the meat from the leftover wings and shred it.
- Mix the shredded chicken with butter, salt, and pepper.
- Stuff the baked potatoes with the seasoned chicken.
- Top with sour cream, shredded cheddar cheese, and chopped green onions.
- Place under the broiler for a few minutes until the cheese melts and the toppings are heated through.

C. Wing Caesar Salad

Ingredients:

- **Leftover BBQ chicken wings**
- **Romaine lettuce, chopped**
- **Caesar dressing**
- **Croutons**
- **Shaved Parmesan cheese**
- **Lemon wedges**

Instructions:

- Remove the meat from the leftover wings and cut into bite-sized pieces.
- Toss the chopped romaine lettuce with Caesar dressing in a bowl.
- Add the wing meat to the salad and mix well.
- Top with croutons and shaved Parmesan cheese.
- Serve with lemon wedges for an extra burst of freshness.

These leftover remix ideas transform your BBQ chicken wings into new and exciting dishes, ensuring that no delicious bite goes to waste. Enjoy the creativity in the kitchen!

Chapter (14) Wing Challenges

A. Spicy Wing Challenge

Spicy Sauce Options:

Prepare an array of spicy wing sauces with varying heat levels. Include classics like buffalo, habanero, ghost pepper, and even create a signature "super-spicy" concoction.

Scoring System:

Develop a scoring system to rate each participant's tolerance for heat. Consider factors like facial expressions, tears, and verbal reactions. Assign points based on the perceived spiciness of each sauce.

Prizes for the Champion:

Crown the participant who braves the spiciest wings as the "Spice Master." Offer prizes such as a cooling dessert, a soothing drink, or a trophy to commemorate their victory.

B. Blind Taste Test Party

Variety of Flavors:

Prepare an assortment of wings featuring different global flavors, sauces, and rubs. Keep track of each flavor so you can reveal the answers later.

Blindfolds and Mystery Wings:

Blindfold participants and have them taste each wing without knowing the flavor. Encourage them to guess the ingredients or style of each wing.

Score and Guessing Game:

Provide scorecards for participants to rate and guess the flavors. Tally up the scores and declare a winner based on the highest number of correct guesses.

C. Building Your Own Wing Bar

Wing Base:

Offer a variety of wing options, including traditional, boneless, or even cauliflower wings for a vegetarian twist.

Sauces and Rubs:

Create a selection of sauces and rubs inspired by different cuisines. Include classic BBQ, honey mustard, teriyaki, and hot buffalo, among others.

Toppings and Dips:

Set up a topping bar with options like chopped green onions, sesame seeds, shredded cheese, and crumbled blue cheese. Provide a variety of dips such as ranch, blue cheese, and sriracha mayo.

Customization Station:

Allow guests to customize their wings by choosing their preferred sauce, rub, and toppings. This interactive experience adds an element of creativity to the wing-eating festivities.

Whether you're testing heat tolerance, exploring flavor palates, or encouraging creativity, these wing challenges are sure to add a fun and competitive element to your gathering. Enjoy the excitement and camaraderie that comes with a good wing challenge!

Chapter (15) Family-Friendly Wing Night

A. Kid-Friendly Marinades
Honey Garlic Wings:

Marinade the wings in a mixture of honey, soy sauce, minced garlic, and a touch of ketchup. This creates a sweet and savory flavor that kids love.

Mild BBQ Wings:

Choose a mild BBQ sauce or make a homemade version with ketchup, brown sugar, and a dash of Worcestershire sauce. It provides the classic BBQ taste without the heat.

Teriyaki Glazed Wings:

Create a teriyaki marinade using soy sauce, pineapple juice, ginger, and a hint of brown sugar. It's a kid-friendly option with a delicious Asian twist.

B. DIY Wing Decorating Station
Prepared Wings:

Pre-cook a batch of plain or lightly seasoned wings for kids to customize.

Sauce Variety:

Set up a station with an assortment of mild and kid-friendly sauces such as honey mustard, ranch, and mild BBQ.

Toppings and Sprinkles:

Provide fun toppings like grated cheese, chopped scallions, and even colorful sprinkles for a sweet twist.

Brushes and Tongs:

Supply small brushes or tongs for kids to apply their chosen sauces and toppings. This adds an interactive and creative element to the meal.

C. Movie Night with Wings
Cozy Setup:

Create a comfortable movie night space with blankets and cushions. Set up a projector or choose a family-favorite film.

Wing Baskets:

Serve the kid-friendly wings in individual baskets or bowls, making it easy for everyone to grab their share.

Dipping Station:

Include a dipping station with kid-friendly sauces like ketchup, ranch, or a mild cheese dip.

Snack Platter:

Accompany the wings with a platter of kid-friendly snacks such as carrot sticks, celery, and fruit slices.

Dessert:

Cap off the night with a sweet treat, whether it's popcorn, cookies, or ice cream sundaes. Create a dessert station for the family to enjoy during the movie.

This family-friendly wing night combines tasty flavors, creative activities, and the joy of a movie night for a memorable and enjoyable experience for everyone. Enjoy the quality time and delicious wings with your loved ones!

Chapter (16) Wing Etiquette

A. Proper Wing Eating Techniques
Hold and Twist:

Grasp the chicken wing at the thickest end. Give it a gentle twist to separate the drumette from the wingette easily.

Clean Bite:

Take a clean bite by pulling the meat away from the bone with your teeth. Avoid gnawing on the bone directly.

Avoid Double-Dipping:

When using communal dipping sauces, take a small amount onto your plate and dip from there. Avoid double-dipping to maintain hygiene.

Napkin Usage:

Keep a napkin handy to wipe your hands as needed. However, it's generally acceptable to have slightly messy fingers during a wing feast.

B. Finger-Licking Etiquette
Mindful Licking:
If you enjoy the flavors on your fingers, do so discreetly. A subtle lick is acceptable, but avoid excessive finger-licking in a formal setting.

Use Napkins:
Prioritize napkins for cleaning your fingers. Licking can be seen as less refined in certain settings, so opting for napkins is the safer choice.

Handwashing:
After the wing feast, excuse yourself to wash your hands thoroughly, especially if you've indulged in finger-licking.

C. Hosting a Wing Night Gathering
Provide Ample Napkins:
Wings can be messy, so ensure you have an abundance of napkins available for guests to use.

Diverse Sauces:
Offer a variety of sauces to accommodate different preferences. This adds an element of choice and excitement to the gathering.

Wet Wipes or Damp Towels:
Have wet wipes or damp towels available for guests who may prefer a more thorough cleanup, especially if finger-licking is encouraged.

Trash Receptacles:
Place strategically located trash receptacles for guests to dispose of bones and used napkins easily.

Seating Arrangements:
If possible, arrange seating to allow for comfortable wing consumption. This might involve providing extra table space or ensuring ample room for finger-licking enthusiasts.

Remember, the most important aspect of a wing night gathering is the enjoyment and camaraderie. Encourage guests to relax and savor the delicious flavors without worrying too much about etiquette.

Chapter (17) Behind the Grill: BBQ Chicken Wing Stories

A. Personal Stories from Grill Enthusiasts

Backyard Grilling Triumphs:

Share stories of backyard grilling triumphs, where enthusiasts experimented with marinades, rubs, and cooking techniques to create the perfect batch of BBQ chicken wings.

Wing Competitions:

Narrate experiences of participating in wing competitions, from friendly neighborhood contests to larger events. Highlight the creativity and camaraderie that comes with these flavorful challenges.

Family Traditions:

Explore family traditions centered around BBQ chicken wings. Whether it's a secret family recipe passed down through generations or a special occasion where wings take center stage, these stories add a personal touch to the BBQ wing narrative.

B. Historic Roots of BBQ Chicken Wings
Buffalo, New York: The Birthplace of Buffalo Wings:
Dive into the history of Buffalo wings, tracing their origin to the Anchor Bar in Buffalo, New York, in 1964. Explore how this iconic dish became a global sensation.
Evolution of Wing Styles:
Explore the evolution of BBQ chicken wings, from classic buffalo to an array of global flavors. Discuss how different cultures and cuisines have influenced the way wings are prepared and enjoyed.
Popularity Surge:
Examine the timeline of BBQ chicken wings' rise to popularity, from local favorites to being featured on menus worldwide. Discuss key moments and trends that contributed to their widespread appeal.
C. Wing Festivals Around the World
National Buffalo Wing Festival (Buffalo, USA):
Explore the National Buffalo Wing Festival, an annual event featuring wing-eating contests, live music, and a celebration of all things Buffalo wings.

London Wing Fest (London, UK):
Highlight the London Wing Fest, a festival bringing together top wing vendors to compete for the title of the best wings in the city. Discuss the cultural exchange of flavors and techniques.
The Great Aussie BBQ Festival (Australia):
Discuss how BBQ chicken wings have made their mark in Australian BBQ culture, with festivals like The Great Aussie BBQ Festival showcasing the best of local grilling traditions.
Sharing personal stories, exploring the historical roots of BBQ chicken wings, and delving into wing festivals around the world add depth and context to the beloved dish. These narratives connect people through a shared love of good food and the joy of grilling.

Chapter (18) Wing Photography and Presentation

A. Tips for Capturing Mouthwatering Wing Photos

Natural Lighting:

Utilize natural light to showcase the vibrant colors and textures of your wings. Photograph near a window during the daytime or choose well-lit outdoor settings.

Close-ups for Detail:

Capture close-up shots to highlight the details of the wings, such as the crispy skin, charred edges, and glossy glaze. Get up close to showcase the mouthwatering texture.

Angles and Perspectives:

Experiment with different angles and perspectives to add visual interest. Capture shots from above, at eye level, or even from a slightly skewed angle for dynamic compositions.

Background Selection:

Choose backgrounds that complement the colors of the wings. Neutral tones or contrasting textures can enhance the visual appeal of your photos.

Action Shots:

Capture action shots of sauce drizzling or wings being pulled apart. These shots add a dynamic element and convey the irresistible nature of the dish.

B. Plating Techniques for Instagram-Worthy Wings

Colorful Accents:

Use colorful garnishes like fresh herbs, sliced citrus, or vibrant vegetables to add a pop of color to your plate. This creates an eye-catching contrast with the wings.

Contrasting Textures:

Consider serving wings on textured plates or cutting boards to enhance the visual appeal. The contrast between the crispy wings and the surface they're placed on can be visually stimulating.

Sauces in Drizzle Patterns:

Drizzle sauces in artistic patterns on the plate to create an appealing visual design. This not only looks great but also showcases the variety of flavors.

Symmetry and Balance:

Arrange wings symmetrically or in a balanced composition for a polished and organized presentation. This makes your photo more visually pleasing.

Use Props Sparingly:

Integrate props that complement the theme, but use them sparingly. The focus should remain on the wings. Simple props like rustic utensils or a linen napkin can add a touch of sophistication.

C. Creating a Wing Presentation Board

Wooden or Slate Boards:

Use wooden or slate boards as a base for presenting your wings. These materials add a rustic and visually appealing backdrop.

Individual Serving Bowls:

Arrange wings in individual serving bowls for a neat and organized presentation. This also allows you to showcase different sauces or flavors separately.

Garnish with Fresh Herbs:

Garnish the presentation board with fresh herbs like parsley, cilantro, or chives. The greenery adds a touch of freshness and elevates the overall look.

Strategic Placement:

Place the wings strategically on the board, leaving enough space between each piece. This ensures that each wing is visible and doesn't overcrowd the presentation.

Capturing Overhead Shots:

If your presentation is on a flat surface, capture stunning overhead shots to showcase the entire spread. Ensure even lighting to capture all the details.

By implementing these tips, your wing photography and presentation can turn a delicious dish into a visually captivating experience for your audience. Whether sharing on social media or creating a visual feast for guests, attention to detail makes all the difference.

Chapter (19) Holiday Wing Specials

A. Festive Wing Recipes for Thanksgiving and Christmas

Cranberry Glazed Wings:

Prepare a glaze using cranberry sauce, orange zest, honey, and a touch of cinnamon. Brush it on the wings before baking or grilling for a festive touch.

Herb-Roasted Turkey Wings:

Marinate wings in a mixture of olive oil, garlic, rosemary, and thyme. Roast them until golden brown for a taste reminiscent of Thanksgiving turkey.

Cider-Bourbon Glazed Wings:

Create a glaze using apple cider, bourbon, brown sugar, and a hint of Dijon mustard. Brush it on the wings and bake or grill to perfection.

B. New Year's Eve Wing Party Ideas

Champagne Glazed Wings:

Combine champagne, honey, and a splash of citrus for a luxurious glaze. Bake or grill the wings and finish with a sprinkle of edible gold dust for a New Year's Eve touch.

Party-Size Wing Platter:

Create a variety of wing flavors to cater to different tastes. Include classics like buffalo, teriyaki, and garlic parmesan for a crowd-pleasing assortment.

Festive Dipping Sauces:

Elevate your wings with gourmet dipping sauces such as truffle aioli, mango habanero, or tzatziki. Provide a selection for guests to choose from.

Countdown Wing Clock:

Arrange wings on a platter in the shape of a clock with each flavor representing an hour. As the clock strikes midnight, guests can enjoy a new flavor.

C. Fourth of July BBQ Extravaganza

Red, White, and Blue Wings:

Create a patriotic theme by using blue cheese dressing, red hot sauce, and white ranch as dipping sauces. Arrange the wings in the shape of the American flag for a festive display.

BBQ Bacon-Wrapped Wings:

Wrap wings with bacon before grilling or baking, adding a smoky flavor. Glaze with BBQ sauce for an irresistible combination of flavors.

Firework Marinade:

Infuse wings with a spicy marinade featuring cayenne pepper, chili powder, and a splash of hot sauce. The heat mimics the excitement of Fourth of July fireworks.

Summer Sides:

Serve wings with classic summer sides like grilled corn on the cob, watermelon salad, and coleslaw to create a full BBQ experience.

Whether it's Thanksgiving, Christmas, New Year's Eve, or the Fourth of July, these holiday wing specials add a festive and delicious touch to your celebrations. Tailor the flavors to match the season and create memorable moments with family and friends.

Chapter (19) Future Wing Trends

A. Emerging Flavors and Techniques

Global Fusion Wings:

Expect to see wings infused with diverse global flavors, from Middle Eastern za'atar to Korean gochujang. Chefs will continue to experiment with international spices and techniques.

Plant-Based Wings:

As plant-based eating gains popularity, anticipate a surge in creative plant-based wing options. These could include cauliflower wings, tempeh wings, or innovative creations using alternative proteins.

Bold Heat Profiles:

The quest for unique heat experiences will drive the creation of wings with intensified spiciness. Whether through exotic chili blends or proprietary hot sauces, wings will push the boundaries of heat.

B. Wing Fusion Cuisine

Wing Tacos and Wraps:

Fusion cuisine will bring about the marriage of wings and wraps, creating tantalizing options like wing tacos with unique slaws, salsas, and sauces.

Wing Sushi Rolls:

Imagine sushi rolls featuring crispy wings as a central element. The combination of textures and flavors will provide a delightful twist on traditional sushi.

Wing Ramen and Noodle Bowls:

Wings will find their way into comforting noodle bowls, adding protein and flavor to ramen, udon, and other noodle-based dishes.

C. DIY Wing Kits and Subscription Boxes

Home Wing Experiences:

DIY wing kits will become popular, allowing enthusiasts to recreate restaurant-quality wings at home. These kits may include pre-marinated wings, signature sauces, and easy-to-follow cooking instructions.

Subscription Box Adventures:

Wing subscription boxes will offer curated monthly experiences, introducing subscribers to new flavors, sauces, and cooking techniques. Each box may include a variety of wing styles, from classic to innovative.

Virtual Wing Tasting Events:

Expect virtual wing tasting events where subscribers join online gatherings to taste and discuss unique wing creations. This trend will foster a sense of community among wing enthusiasts worldwide.

The future of wing trends is exciting, promising a diverse array of flavors, innovative fusions, and interactive experiences for wing lovers. As culinary boundaries continue to expand, so too will the possibilities for reinventing this beloved dish.

Chapter (20) Wing-Themed Beverages

A. Wing and Beer Pairing Guide

Classic Buffalo Wings with Pale Ale:

The hoppy bitterness of a pale ale complements the tangy heat of classic buffalo wings. The effervescence helps cut through the richness of the sauce.

Honey Mustard Wings with Wheat Beer:

The light and slightly sweet profile of a wheat beer pairs well with the honey mustard glaze on the wings. The refreshing quality enhances the overall dining experience.

Barbecue Wings with Brown Ale:

Brown ales with their malty sweetness and nutty undertones complement the smoky flavors of barbecue wings. The caramel notes provide a delightful contrast.

Teriyaki Wings with IPA:

The bold and hoppy characteristics of an IPA stand up well to the savory and sweet notes of teriyaki wings, creating a robust and flavorful combination.

Garlic Parmesan Wings with Pilsner:

The crispness of a pilsner works beautifully with the garlic parmesan coating, cleansing the palate between bites and enhancing the savory elements.

B. DIY Wing-Infused Cocktails

Buffalo Caesar Cocktail:

Ingredients:

- 2 oz vodka
- 1 oz clamato juice
- 1/2 oz hot sauce

- **Dash of Worcestershire sauce**

Instructions:
Rim the glass with buffalo wing seasoning. Shake all ingredients with ice and strain into the glass. Garnish with a celery stick.
Honey Mustard Whiskey Sour:
Ingredients:

- **2 oz whiskey**
- **3/4 oz lemon juice**
- **1/2 oz honey**
- **1/4 oz Dijon mustard**

Instructions:
Shake all ingredients with ice and strain into a glass. Garnish with a lemon twist.
Teriyaki Tea Collins:
Ingredients:

- **2 oz gin**
- **1 oz teriyaki sauce**
- **3/4 oz simple syrup**
- **1 oz fresh lemon juice**
- **Soda water**

Instructions:
Shake gin, teriyaki sauce, simple syrup, and lemon juice with ice. Strain into a glass with ice and top with soda water.
C. Non-Alcoholic Wing-Friendly Drinks
Citrus Infusion Sparkler:
Ingredients:

- **Orange slices**
- **Lemon slices**
- **Lime slices**
- **Sparkling water**

Instructions:

Infuse the water with citrus slices for a refreshing and non-alcoholic palate cleanser.

Iced Mint Green Tea:

Ingredients:

- **Green tea bags**
- **Fresh mint leaves**
- **Honey or agave syrup (optional)**

Instructions:

Brew green tea, add fresh mint leaves, and let it cool. Serve over ice for a crisp and flavorful beverage.

Ginger Beer Fizz:

Ingredients:

- **Ginger beer**
- **Lime juice**
- **Simple syrup (optional)**

Instructions:

Mix ginger beer with fresh lime juice and simple syrup if desired. Serve over ice for a zesty and non-alcoholic option.

These wing-themed beverages add an extra layer of enjoyment to your wing-eating experience, whether you prefer classic pairings, inventive cocktails, or non-alcoholic options. Cheers to a delightful feast!

Chapter (21) Interactive Cooking Classes

A. Hosting a Virtual Wing Cooking Class

Ingredient Prep Session:

Guide participants through the preparation of essential ingredients, ensuring everyone is ready to dive into the cooking process.

Live Demonstration:

Conduct a live cooking demonstration, showcasing each step of the wing-making process. Offer tips and insights to enhance the cooking experience.

Interactive Q&A:

Create a dynamic atmosphere by encouraging participants to ask questions in real-time. Address queries about techniques, flavor profiles, or alternative ingredient options.

Virtual Tasting Session:

Have participants taste their creations together, fostering a shared experience despite being physically apart. Discuss flavors, textures, and personal touches added during the cooking process.

Recipe Sharing and Feedback:

Conclude the class by inviting participants to share their final dishes and discuss their unique twists on the recipe. Provide constructive feedback and celebrate the diversity of flavors within the virtual cooking community.

B. Team Building Wing Competitions

Wing Recipe Challenge:

Divide participants into teams and challenge them to create a unique wing recipe. Encourage creativity by incorporating specific ingredients or themes.

Speed Wing Cooking Contest:

Set a time limit for teams to cook a set number of wings. Emphasize collaboration, communication, and effective time management to build teamwork.

Judging Panel:

Appoint a judging panel, either within the team or external members, to evaluate the wings based on taste, presentation, and creativity. Provide constructive feedback to enhance the learning experience.

Team Bonding Activities:

Integrate team bonding activities between cooking stages to foster a sense of camaraderie. These could include virtual icebreakers or short challenges to keep the energy high.

Virtual Awards Ceremony:

Conclude the competition with a virtual awards ceremony, recognizing teams for their achievements. Categories can include "Best Flavor," "Most Creative," or "Team Spirit."

C. Wing Tasting Events and Judging Criteria

Tasting Event Setup:

Organize a virtual wing tasting event where participants cook and share their favorite wing recipes. Set up a virtual platform for participants to present their dishes.

Judging Criteria:

Establish clear judging criteria, including flavor, texture, presentation, and creativity. Encourage participants to focus on these aspects when preparing and presenting their wings.

Guest Judges or Peer Evaluation:

Consider having guest judges with culinary expertise or allow participants to evaluate each other's creations. This adds an interactive element to the event and promotes a sense of community.

Public Voting:

Incorporate public voting if the event is open to a wider audience. This can be done through social media polls or a designated voting platform.

Prizes and Recognition:

Recognize winners in various categories and offer virtual prizes or certificates. Celebrate the diverse talents and contributions of participants in the virtual wing-tasting community.

Hosting interactive cooking classes, team building wing competitions, and virtual wing-tasting events adds a delightful and engaging dimension to the culinary experience. These activities bring people together to celebrate their love for wings, fostering connection and shared enjoyment.

❖ Conclusion

A. Recap of Key Points

✓ In the exploration of "Flavors of the Grill: A Crispy BBQ Chicken Wings Adventure," we've covered a range of topics to enhance your wing-cooking journey:

✓ Introduction: Welcomed you to the crispy world of BBQ chicken wings and explained the appeal.

✓ Getting Started: Detailed the essential ingredients and equipment for wing perfection.

✓ Preparing the Wings: Discussed the crucial steps of cleaning, marinating, and applying the rub.

✓ Cooking Methods: Explored grilling and oven-baking techniques for achieving crispy wings.

✓ Basting and Glazing: Emphasized the importance of basting and provided DIY BBQ sauce recipes.

✓ Serving Suggestions: Shared presentation tips and delectable side dishes to accompany your wings.

✓ Troubleshooting: Addressed common issues and provided tips for success.

✓ Variations: Explored creative twists such as smoked wings, Asian-inspired glazes, and dry rub variations.

✓ Appetizer Inspiration: Presented exciting appetizer ideas like Buffalo Chicken Dip, Stuffed Jalapeños, and Chicken Wing Sliders.

✓ Marinade Madness: Unleashed citrus-infused, beer and honey, and teriyaki marinade options.

✓ Wing Hacks and Pro Tips: Shared insider tips for extra crispiness, perfect beer pairings, and grilling secrets.

✓ Healthier Alternatives: Discussed baked vs. fried options and provided alternatives for dietary preferences.

✓ Global Wing Flavors: Took a culinary trip with Caribbean Jerk, Tandoori Spiced, and Mexican Mole Wings.

✓ Leftover Remix: Showcased creative ways to repurpose leftover wings into new and exciting dishes.

✓ Wing Challenges: Introduced spicy challenges, blind taste tests, and DIY wing bars for interactive wing-themed events.

✓ Family-Friendly Wing Night: Tailored wing recipes and activities for a family-friendly, enjoyable evening.

✓ Wing Etiquette: Shared tips on proper wing-eating techniques, finger-licking etiquette, and hosting a wing night gathering.

✓ Behind the Grill: Explored personal stories, the historical roots of BBQ chicken wings, and wing festivals around the world.

✓ Wing Photography and Presentation: Provided guidance on capturing mouthwatering wing photos, plating techniques, and creating a wing presentation board.

✓ Holiday Wing Specials: Offered festive wing recipes for Thanksgiving, Christmas, New Year's Eve, and the Fourth of July.

✓ Future Wing Trends: Previewed emerging flavors, fusion cuisine, and the rise of DIY wing kits and subscription boxes.

✓ Wing-Themed Beverages: Explored beer pairings, DIY wing-infused cocktails, and non-alcoholic options to complement your wings and enhance the overall dining experience.

B. Encouragement to Experiment

As you embark on your BBQ chicken wing adventure, remember that experimentation is key. Feel free to tweak recipes, create your own signature sauces, and explore unique flavor combinations. The world of wings is vast, and your culinary journey is a canvas waiting to be painted with delicious, crispy creations.

C. Share Your Creations

Lastly, share your BBQ chicken wing masterpieces! Whether you're a seasoned griller or a novice in the kitchen, your creations inspire and connect us through the joy of food. Share your experiences, recipes, and photos with friends, family, and the wider community. Let the crispy adventure continue, and may your wings always be flavorful and perfectly cooked!